historia
magistra vitae

Francesco Sisci

A BRAVE NEW CHINA
THE BIG CHANGE

goWare

First published in September 2014
By goWare
Via Reginaldo Giuliani, 88
Firenze, Italy

By agreement with Enrico Lanfranchi

ISBN 978-88-6797-234-0

Foreword

This book is a very modest and painstaking attempt to address something very large. In fact, it is so large that most of us can't or don't want to address it in our short- or long-term future, and yet it is having a growing impact on everything in our lives.

At the forefront of this rise is China, the largest and most different nation from the West, yet others are following. The Indians are trailing not much behind, then there is Southeast Asia, then possibly Africa, and then God knows where else. The first reaction in the West may naturally be—and has been—to try to stop the rise of those civilizations, although the phenomenon was triggered and supported by a series of mainly American policy decisions. Yet at this stage, to reverse the course and stop this rise could be extremely hard, and even if achieved, it would be extremely costly for the West to the point that even a "victory" over the rising nations would destroy the West anyway.

There is also the other side of the coin. Even if the rising nations were to defeat the West by resisting, this victory would be immensely costly for them, so much so that it would condemn the rising nations and the world to centuries of poverty and underdevelopment. The tribes who sacked Rome vanquished their oppressor, but at the same time condemned themselves and the world they conquered to centuries of barbarity. A conflict here has no winners, only losers.

The proposed book, hopefully the first of a series, begins to tackle these problems, which, some readers will know, has been the focus of my work for the past 20 years.

This book is intended for both worlds, the old one of Western countries and that of the rising nations. Its focus is mainly on China, as the biggest and fastest nation on the move. However, the implications go well beyond China, which is not alone in its rise and its problems in this world, but surely, China being so different from anywhere else, shows the present problems in the most extreme form.

The present work will deal with two sets of issues, the various international problems and China's internal issues and transformations. There is a close link between the two, and wrong assessments on either issue can lead to big mistakes with very grave consequences. Here the first thing is to gauge the fundamentals: who are the Chinese now?

The answer to this is not obvious at all to both Chinese and non-Chinese. Both Chinese and outsiders often think of China with misconceptions. This is normal: a man of 54, like myself now, still thinks of himself as a man of 30 or even younger. Consciousness of change always comes well after the change has actually occurred.

For me, the awareness of a change in China came pretty early. I was studying ancient China, but when I actually went to China in the 1980s, I found it very different from the texts I had read. This was especially true coming from Italy, where ruins stretching back to Greek times, some 3,000 years ago, are visible in most towns. In the late 1980s in the People's Republic, there was next to nothing of the ancient China I studied, and by the early 1990s, the Chinese were eager to destroy all that was left of even the old China, houses and monuments dating back "only" four or five centuries.

Moreover, I stumbled in a very interesting volume written at the turn of the past century and published in the year 1900: Things Chinese by James Dyer Ball. It described late 19th–century Chinese customs such as social rules about appointments, weddings, funerals, keeping time, dress codes, housing, and family relations. To me the book gave words to an indescribable perception I had that almost nothing of those social rules applied to China less than a century later.

China in a few decades had transformed in a far more dramatic way than any Western country. For instance, social rules, habits, and dress in Southern Italy—where I was born and grew up and where modernization came late and in a very dramatic way in the 1990s—were basically kept intact. Norms and behaviors then were basically the same as a hundred years before. This was unlike in China where Ball's descriptions seemed to belong to an ancient history museum, to an alien planet of a science fiction book, like Mars.

Still, there is one more leaf. China has changed and is changing, but it is not becoming a blind copy of its Western models, something that can never happen for many reasons. It is becoming something else altogether. The book will start looking at what it is becoming and the implications of this change for China and the world.

Despite the heavy and boring premise, I hope the work will be an easy and intriguing read.

For this volume, I would like here to thank Charles Horner and the Hudson Foundation, which gave me the initial support and inspiration for this enquiry. I would also like to thank old friends and fellow students Lu Xiang and Zhao Tingyang for sharing philosophical conversations and observations about these issues.

The big China change

People's Republic of *China* (PRC) is no longer "old China", it is turning into something very new. America also will be crucial for the end result.

University libraries are filled with thousands of volumes explaining to us and the world all the problems and intricacies of the momentous passage from agricultural to industrial society, from rural to urban life, from a world marked by huge gaps in time and space to another where communications and telecommunications immensely narrow times and distances. These changes still puzzle us and seem largely unexplained. Yet these changes, occurring over a span of 200 years, are minimal if compared to what has been occurring in China in past 30 years.

These changes have been concentrated in a bit more than one generation. But this is just a small part of a larger phenomenon: in the past 150 years, China's complex cultural values have been under constant attack and forced revision. That is, not only did China have to undergo the same structural changes as the West in a shorter period of time, but at the same time, it also underwent dramatic cultural changes. The only similar experiment took place in Japan in the late 19th century. But to put it very briefly, Japan was at much earlier phase of cultural evolution, so the breadth of the structural change was not as huge; it was in a society that claimed it had already absorbed and digested a foreign culture, that of China about a thousand years earlier, so the present digestion of Western culture was within the Japanese tradition; and it could do so with great confidence because in the first phases of the reform, it had military victories over the regional superpower China, in 1894, and a Western power, Russia, in 1905.

China, conversely, arrived to the fast phase of modernization pretty late, with a larger gap to fill in less time. China also didn't have much confidence, as it had been defeated by foreign powers, invaded and almost totally conquered by Japan, and had won only a small war against India. It managed to gain an almost honorable draw with America in Korea in 1950s (with Russian support) and with Vietnam in 1979 (with some American assistance). Furthermore, China had no affirmed tradition of digesting foreign culture into its own mold and changing itself in the process. It has the opposite tradition, of making foreigners "Chinese," which occurred several times in Chinese history. The last time was with the Manchu invaders who eventually were completely Sinified. One could argue that Buddhism vastly changed China, but the current perception is that, in fact, China changed Buddhism even more. Now, the situation is completely different, and there is no doubt that China is changing to adapt to a Western values-dominated world, rather than the contrary.

The country that faced the "foreign devils from the ocean," *yang guizi*, during the Opium Wars in the mid 19th century has dramatically changed in the following century and half – to the point that contemporary China can be regarded as only superficially similar to the country it was during the Opium Wars. In fact, the whole social and personal context, which defines and influences ideas, ambitions, and world-views, has been totally transformed in these 150 years.

1. The new family

The change started with the family, the basis for society and the State. The ideal family in the 19th century was unchanged from the times of Confucius, some 2,000 years before: three generations under one roof. The older man had many wives even more children. Each male heir had also many wives and children all living together harmoniously in a large courtyard, resembling a small village of dozens of people. In the courtyard, there were also many servants. The females of the clan were betrothed to neighbors, who then gained a closer relationship with the family. In this way, whole towns were under the control of one family. Each relative had a name indicating his precise relationship to the speaker. There were no vague appellations like "aunt," "uncle" or "cousin." There were terms such as "uncle, first younger brother of my father" (*da shushu*) or "uncle, second brother of my mother" (*er jiu-jiu*), and so on. Cousins also bore different names, accordingly. It was an intricate cobweb of relations in which each individual had his or her precise place. A male child grew up thinking that if he studied hard and if he were virtuous and filial, he would pass the official exam, become a successful mandarin, inherit the family fortune, and establish his own large family home. Then, he would pick the brightest of his heirs and support that child through his studies, continuing the glorious family tradition.

That was an ideal. Most men had only one wife, as they could afford only one. Some men, poor, had no wives; and some, just a little less poor, had to share a wife with their brothers. Yet, the ideal family was one man, many wives and many, many children.

For the emperor, this condition was an issue of State security. The emperor had many wives to make sure he had many children and could choose the fittest among them to succeed him. The successor had to be male, but not necessarily the first born from the first wife, as was the situation in Europe. The Chinese system tried to make sure the emperor was not incompetent, which could be the case with the European system where God chose the successor – namely, the first born. The issue of family and keeping only one wife was the stumbling block in the conversion of the Qing emperor to Catholicism.

The emperor might have entertained the idea of converting to Catholicism, as many of his closest advisors were Jesuits, but he could not accept the idea of having one wife, as this would alter the rule for succession in China. However, the Jesuits in the 17th century knew that they could not compromise on the rule of succession: the king's many wives and their children had been the very issue that caused a split between England and Rome the century before with Henry VIII and Elizabeth. Elizabeth died in 1603, seven years before Matteo Ricci's demise in Beijing in 1610.

This ideal of the family persisted until the Communists took over in 1949. After the May 4th movement in 1919, the idea of one wife was introduced as progressive and modern. However, Chiang Kai-shek had more than one wife, as did many senior KMT officials. Conversely, the Communist party broke the old mold and introduced puritanical rules imposing just one wife. This was already a major break with the ancient tradition, but an even greater break came in the 1980s with the one-child rule. This completely reversed the old pyramid of relations. A hundred years before, a grandfather could be served by scores of grandchildren all vying for his favor.

In 1980s, one couple, often two single children of single-wife marriages, could have as many as four grandparents all hovering around a single child. Then, one has six adults spoiling one child. It is the phenomenon of the "little emperors." The children were spoiled, but also under enormous pressure. They had the responsibility to succeed for their family's glory. In larger families, this responsibility was spread among scores of siblings who first had to learn to live with each other. In 1980s, the one child had to be number one in his class to be sure to get into a good high school, which, in turn, guarantees a place at a good university in the extremely selective Chinese education system. But this, of course, is impossible. What happens, then, in most families, if the one child fails to get into a good university and has no hope for a good job? How will the children reconcile themselves with their lot? Will they be frustrated and angry? They are no small number – there are millions of children in this generation. How will these people impact the society, State, world, and culture in the next 20 years?

One thing is sure, China has never experienced a generation like this, and neither has any place else in the world, so it is very hard to forecast trends. Because the situation is so widespread, the Chinese government has realized the problem and is trying to address it. But before turning our attention to the answer, first we have to look at how the Chinese government has dramatically changed.

2. End to the emperor

Since unification in the late 3ʳᵈ century BC, China was always ruled by an emperor, a supreme head of State, ultimate source of power, and decision-maker. Possibly, there had been "emperors" even before then, such as the son of heaven (*tianzi*) of Zhou times, but he was likely more of a religious and ceremonial figure than a real political monarch.

The imperial system really started with the first emperor, Qinshi Huangdi. The system underwent many changes, but there was always one constant element: the monarch did not run the administration of the country. That duty was largely entrusted to a body of ministers and officials who were selected on the basis of merit. The emperor embodied the interest of the State, as the State was his. It was a mechanism similar to that of modern companies differentiating property and management. The owner, or major stock-holder, sets the goals and decides the broad direction and the interests of the company, such as its stability and welfare. The emperor's interests coincide with the interests of the population, or in our comparison, the employees in a company. The citizens want to lead comfortable safe lives, and creating this environment maintains with a stable hold on power for the emperor.

In the middle, between the emperor and the people, there were officials who had the job of running the country and maintaining stability. It is easy to see how people recognized their interests as coinciding with those of the emperor, and thus, both the emperor and the people blamed officials if something minor went wrong. If something major was wrong, it meant the emperor had lost his marbles, he did not understand his and his people's interests, or heaven did not want him to rule – and that was the end for him and the dynasty. They would be replaced by a new emperor and dynasty, setting new standards for the old stability game.

In the 19th century, Chiang Kai-shek and Mao Zedong also followed this pattern. Although they did not call themselves "emperor," they were the ultimate embodiment of the interests of the State and the ones who set the grand directions. Deng Xiaoping's rule was softer, but he still commanded great respect. Jiang Zemin was something in between. However, the real radical change occurred right at the beginning of this century, with the smooth transition of power from Jiang Zemin to Hu Jintao. That transition confirmed that both men were not emperors. They are officials promoted because of merit to become head of State, but they do not embody the ultimate interests of the State. They cannot make the ultimate decisions alone – they have to reach a consensus among top leaders. And they cannot even choose their own successors: Hu's post was decided by Deng (Jiang might have preferred Zeng Qinghong), and Hu's successor Xi Jinping was not decided by Hu alone (who might have preferred Li Keqiang). Both Jiang and Hu are top managers, but this poses a new question: who embodies the interests of the State and of the people?

In democracies, those interests are represented by the electoral body, which votes for the head of State and other representatives. In modern China, there are no elections and the "legitimization" offered by the leaders is simple: we are in power because we are in power. If nobody topples us, then we are legitimized to stay. We can stay in power by granting economic growth and development that spreads welfare to the whole population, although unequally.

However, legitimization is only part of the issue. The larger issue is: who decides the broad direction to take? What are the criteria and standards to judge the performance of officials and top managing-rulers? Here, there are two arenas that have a greater and lesser voice in deciding the performance and setting the goals.

The less powerful arena (whose voice is growing) is public opinion, which is conveyed by a number of channels, such as local media, blogs on the web, social surveys, and local elections. This does not form a black and white picture but reveals where the general interests are moving or not moving. For instance, on the issue of environmental protection, ten years ago people were less responsive to it, but now they are more receptive.

A more powerful arena influencing the leaders is the pool of experts, old cadres called on to discuss different policies. The opinion of experts is solicited when considering any given policy, and the opinion of retired cadres, who now have no vested interests, is also called on to consider the promotion of officials. Tens of thousands were consulted to draw the program for the last party congress in 2007, and 5,000 helped write the draft. Even after retirement, officials have access to some levels of internal news bulletins and maintain privileged channels of communication with top leadership. Therefore, they influence the broad decision process. But the system is not transparent, leading to all possible venues for corruption. For example, middle- and low-level officials who are backed by companies can try to climb up the official ladder by distributing presents and favors to higher-ranking officials. Companies, especially if they are State companies, can try to move policies by offering gifts and favors to officials.

To counter these instances, the party has moved toward appealing to scholarly experts, with no personal interest in the issues, and retired cadres, also without personal interests. They also keep the process secretive and thus not open to wide interference. But even this system is not tight – and they know it. For this reason, they are now pushing for democratization, although they are concerned about the shortcomings of that system, as well.

The party is currently facing a major quandary about how to move forward – and also because, for most people, the ultimate goal is to be emperor.

3. A crowd of emperors

Right at the end of Tiananmen Square, next to Zhengyangmen ("the Midday gate") and two hundred meters from Mao's mausoleum, there is a spot where people can take pictures of their children dressed as little Manchu emperors and sitting on a throne. The place is symbolic: the ancient gate once opened on the nei cheng (the inner city) and the buildings of the imperial government. Every day, there is a line of parents, mostly from the countryside, holding their children by the hands and waiting to take the picture as a sign of good luck. Each parent wants his or her only child to be successful – to become, in his or her way, an emperor.

For centuries in ancient times, there were only two ways to be successful.

The first way was to lead a rebellion or follow one – to topple the dynasty and become the emperor. This was the method of Liu Bang (the founder of the Han dynasty), Zhu Yuanzhang (the founder of the Ming dynasty), and Mao Zedong (the founder of the "Communist dynasty"). The path is extremely dangerous – one could easily lose his head over it – and possibilities of success are very slim.

Second, an ambitious young man could pursue a career as an imperial official. He could take the challenging exams, and if he passed them, become even the top official of the empire. This path had no risk – nobody would kill the failed youth who did not pass the exam. And it was relatively easier. Although the official bureaucracy was tiny compared to the population, there were still hundreds of officials to be promoted every year, giving the average person a much better chance to succeed this way than by rebelling against the system. For this reason, most people first tried to become an official.

However, the exam system was not perfect, and many rebel leaders began as students who had failed the imperial examinations, like the famous Hong Xiuquan who started the Taiping rebellion that in the middle of the 19th century, an uprising that almost toppled the Qing dynasty. If these brilliant people had earned a post, perhaps there would have been no rebellion or a much more modest one.

Actually, there was also a less common path to try to make a fortune for oneself – clever people could go into business. This path, however, was not as glorious as the choice of being an official, the top of the social hierarchy. And although not as risky as being a rebel, it was far from secure. In fact, officials could easily concoct all kinds of excuses to seize the property of rich merchants. Business, concentrated in cities, was tolerated but not exalted, and businessmen had to be careful not to eclipse the wealth of local officials, who had to remain officially the richest in the area. Businessmen could protect their assets in two ways: befriending the officials or having his son pass the examination and become an official. The second choice was safer and considered more socially respectable than the first.

The rest of people, the vast majority of the population, were peasants who were bound to the land and had all types of constraints to leaving his place and moving somewhere else. Furthermore, officials and peasants were the stronghold of stable power, the guarantors that nothing would change and the imperial power would be unchallenged. Business, with its drive to accumulate wealth and invest in new ventures, was a force for instability and change. This had to be tolerated for several reasons, but the imperial power could not allow business and enterprise to grow to threaten the emperor's stability.

This situation has largely changed in the past 30 years. There are still officials selected through a complex party system with courses and exams, but now business is exalted for the first time in Chinese history. Business is central to the drive for fast development, which is the paramount task for the nation to recover its former might and glory.

This has many consequences.

On a personal level, being a businessman is now as glorious as – or perhaps even more than – being an official. When the best kids at university are chosen to join the party and have an official career, they feel it is an honor that they must accept. But this career is long, very difficult, full of traps, and rewarding only at the end – if, at around age 50, one has managed to survive the political selection and become a senior official.

However, most young people prefer to try to become businessmen. They can be successful early in their lives, they're freer since they're not subject to the strict party discipline, and they can enjoy themselves with the money they make. A businessman can have his own enterprise and decide what to do with minimal official interference. In other words, each young person can become the little emperor of a small empire, something that did not exist in the imperial past. Besides, trying one's hand in business is easier and far less risky than trying to start a revolution to become emperor.

On a social level, the changes brought by business and enterprises must be "digested" at every level by the system. Formerly, the imperial system could stop businesses from threatening the status quo. Now the nation wants to improve the status quo, and therefore has to push for new businesses and then factor in the constant changes to the social and political fabric of the nation. Moreover, business-driven growth means urbanization, depopulation of the countryside, extinction of the old peasants, the end of ancient rural China, and the birth of a new, urbanized China. This course will follow the only existing pattern for urbanization – the Western one.

Most importantly, the overall system has discarded the ancient notion of stability and embraced the notions of change and development. This is a deep cultural change, confirmed by the official Chinese rhetoric about stability. When the leaders stress the need for stability in China, they are looking for some balance in a situation that has inherently rejected it.

And if everything fails, the government thinks, there must be something to appease the public. In the West, those appeasements were traditionally sports and religion.

4. Sporting

Public sporting events, attended by both the aristocratic and common people, have been popular since ancient times in the West. The tradition of the Olympics was that all Greek cities would suspend activities so that the entire population could enjoy the games, an event with the spirit of bringing together all citizens united by a common cultural identity and mutual interests. The spirit of the Roman circus was the same. The patrician and the plebeian would attend it to share in the common enjoyment of the show, and thus, renew the cultural bond linking the two parts of the society. The games had also a link with war, the other crucial occasion where high and low stand side-by-side, this time to shed blood in defense of the common motherland. In Greece, war was suspended during the games; in Rome, games were a recreation of war with fights between gladiators.

Sport thus played a crucial political and ritualistic function in creating a sense of common belonging. This was extremely important as both Greek and Roman societies were split into separate strata on the basis of birthright. In Greece, the aristocrats were concentrated in the upper portion of the city, the acropolis, and the common people had the lower square of the "agora." A similar structure could be found in Rome, where the old aristocrats centered on the Senate and the plebeians would live in the lower strata of the "urbs". Upward movement was possible but very difficult and uncommon.

This social difference, determined by birth, was very hard to overcome and created a huge social gap that the common attendance at games or participation in war helped to bridge.

The system was highly effective. Even now there are families in Rome claiming a lineage back to Julius Cesar, living in the same area and the same buildings for millennia, despite many changes in the ruling elite of the land. The concept of aristocracy, of blue-blood privileges, was very strong for centuries in the West. Apart from the many crowned heads of State in Europe, England's House of Lords is a modern vestige of the old Roman Senate: a group of grandees – largely chosen by the merits of their forefathers – ruling the nation of common people.

In ancient China, there were no games or circus bonding upper and lower strata. However, there were also no birth-determined social divides, and upward mobility based purely on merit had been encouraged and idealized since very ancient times. The Mozi, possibly the earliest text of systematic philosophy in China, begins its earliest part (4th century BC) by discussing the importance of promoting capable people as high officials (Mozi, shang xian pian). The philosopher also claims this is an ancient tradition coming from the Shang dynasty (2nd millennium BC), which in turn was taken from the most legendary ancient Chinese emperors – Yao, Shun, Yi, and Tang – who selected their successors on the basis of merit regardless of origin. In fact, Shun or Yi had very humble origins.

Confucius, about a generation older than Mozi but referring to the earlier cultural tradition of Zhou (starting around 1,000 BC), also stressed the paramount importance of education and upbringing over birthright in the promotion of officials.

The original and enduring Chinese cultural myth is of a self-made man – the senior official born out of a peasant family or the top general starting off as foot soldier. In this sense, social mobility was encouraged, and this may have created a strong bond in society. In fact, as we have seen, there were two channels for upward mobility: the selection of officials, which is open to all, and the revolution (*ge ming*). The second is particularly important in comparison to Western tradition. Since the early first millennium BC, there has been the tradition of the change (*ge*) of the Mandate of Heaven (*ming*). Essentially, the idea was that the dynasty would rule until it was overthrown. The toppling was seen as legitimate when it was successful, evidence that Heaven had withdrawn its graces from one emperor and granted them to another. The emperor, Son of Heaven, had to hold onto its power. His success in so doing proved his ritual and religious legitimacy. Large natural disasters and social uprisings confirmed the waning of Heaven's favors.

Besides the selected officials, each dynasty had its court of aristocrats – relatives of the emperor or descendents of the closest comrades of the founder of the dynasty. They, and the relatives of the senior officials, had varying influence. But this influence faded with the decades, as the generations grew away from the original connection. Furthermore, each change of dynasty completely wiped out the former aristocracy and established a new one. The Mongols eliminated the Song aristocrats, so did the Ming with Mongols, the Manchu with the Ming, and the communists with the Manchu. This created a situation where there is no aristocratic continuity stretching back hundreds of years, as there is in Europe. At most, Chinese aristocrats can claim a lineage of three hundred years. Presently, there is no official aristocracy, but the siblings of senior leaders are called "*taizi dang*" ("princelings"). However, even they can claim an aristocracy that is less than one hundred years old. This means that social mobility is strong, and aristocracy has not played a role as conspicuous and continuous as it has in Europe.

This has also changed. Communists now have started looking to sports – especially mass gatherings like the Olympics that are attended by both common people and senior officials – to create a new social bond. Now, there are more occasions for the people to feel a sense of unity. There are also new and old systems for social mobility (promotion of officials, career opportunities in business), a weak aristocracy, and more occasions of coming together for sports.

The present attention to sports is still weaker than in the West, often because of the extreme corruption in local tournaments. But there is also a phenomenon unknown in Western societies: great attention to sports from abroad. Chinese people love soccer played in Italy, England, Germany, and Spain as well as basketball from the US. This appreciation of foreign sports has also created positive attention for developments abroad, in the countries home of those games, in a way unknown in the West. And it is extending the feeling of unity the Chinese feel with the motherlands of those games.

This is a phenomenon that goes beyond sports.

5. Religion

China traditionally has not had a religious system that is comparable to the monotheistic religions of the West or the polytheistic religions of India and many other countries. There was Buddhist-Taoist lore full of metaphysical explanations for various phenomena. In addition, there was a system of civil values without any metaphysics, which we may call Confucian ethics.

Both of those systems were criticized by modernist intellectuals during 1919's May 4th Movement and were then smashed in Maoist times and replaced with an atheist religion that idolized Mao Zedong. In the early 1980s, at the end of the Maoist era, China was without any kind of values system, either religious or civil.

Since the early 1980s, China has seen a massive return of the traditional Taoist semi-religious respiratory practice of Qigong. Elderly Chinese leaders were eager to practice this discipline, which promised an earthly long life. They arranged the return of Qigong masters (who sometimes were just self-taught), organizing them as sport trainers and registering them under the Sport Federation. There were many Qigong schools flourishing all over the country, and a dozen of them were registered with the Sport Federation.

Their popularity increased after the Tiananmen movement in 1989, when many young people who were disillusioned with politics went into meditation. Furthermore, in early 1995, Deng Xiaoping had a stroke and almost died. He was saved, according to Beijing's rumor mill, by the intervention of revered Qigong masters. This episode helped increase the fame of Qigong.

By the mid-1990s, police, soldiers, officials, and students were all practicing various forms of Qigong. Among them, the most successful was the Falun Gong. It was the best organized with cells, a central committee, and a politburo modeled after the Communist party. Its set of beliefs was a mishmash of old and new: faith in the coming end of the world, the idea that extraterrestrial beings were among us and had taken the shape of men, the denial of modern science and medicine, and a strong xenophobic attitude. The last sentiment well suited the many ageing leaders who had joined the Party in their youth with nationalist sentiments.

The Falun Gong movement grew so strong that it demanded recognition as an official religion and to no longer be classified as a sport. When it failed to obtain that classification, followers organized a series of demonstrations in early 1999 with the support of senior Chinese intelligence and military officers. The government saw these demonstrations – backed by crucial officials – as a powerful threat, an attempted coup d'etat, and commenced a gradual yet merciless crackdown.

This moment was crucial in China for the return of religion. The whole Falun Gong episode convinced the Party that what was formerly believed – that opening up was too much – was not true. In fact, opening up was too little. This had made it possible for millions to believe absurd theories about UFOs or to refuse modern medical attention.

Yet, it also revealed that Chinese people wanted religious values, and the government had to be open to them. Buddhism was favored: it was a religion that had been in China for hundreds of years, Chinese people were very familiar to it, and Buddhist monks had been among the first to denounce the dangers of Falun Gong in 1998.

Furthermore, the Chinese leaders had realized that much-feared Christian faiths were not so dangerous after all. In 50 years of Communist rule, despite ruthless oppression, Christian Protestants and Catholics had never staged demonstrations in Tiananmen, as the Falun Gong followers had. In 1989, during the Tiananmen demonstrations, then-bishop Zen from Hong Kong told students in Chinese seminars not to get involved with the demonstrations.

This created new goodwill among the Chinese leadership for traditional religions and made possible official overtures to the Vatican in 2001 for the normalization of ties with China. In 2001, Pan Yue also wrote an article that redefined the theoretical concept[1]. Pan Yue argued, essentially, that Marx said that religion is the opiate of the people, and thus religion is bad for revolution. But once revolution is successful, the government needs religion as opiate to avert new revolutions. The reasoning is crude but fitting for Chinese political thought. It also changed the meaning of revolution from the original Marxist one, entailing a total change of political order, to the Chinese "*ge ming*," a simple traditional Chinese change of political power.

This brought the momentous change of 2007.

On December 18th, the Politburo of the Communist Party of China (CPC), the highest ruling body in the country, held a plenary collective study session. It was the second one since the Party Congress ended in October. For the first time in the history of the People's Republic, the Party top echelons met to discuss a once-taboo subject – religion.

The CPC, like many other Communist Parties, is patently atheist to the point that religious affiliation is forbidden for Party members. However, right in Congress there was the first sign that things could be moving into a different direction.

Broadcasting from the cavernous Great Hall of the People, where congress was in session, TV screens showed the slim and attentive face of the young Panchen Lama, who was following the speech of the General Secretary Hu Jintao. The badge on his chest said "guest."

The shot revealed that the most important religious dignitary in Tibet was supportive of the Beijing government, and also that the Party was reconsidering its stance on religion. Now religious personalities were invited guests, but perhaps, in a not so distant future, they could also be full-

---

1   Pan Yue on Huaxia Shibao, December 15, 2001. ("Marxist view on religion must keep in step with times.")

fledged delegates to Congress. That is, the Party could drop its ban against religious figures joining its ranks.

In fact, Hu's keynote speech devoted a whole paragraph to religion[2]. He said that religious people, including priests, monks, and lay-believers, played a positive role in the social and economic development of China. Furthermore, Hu did not talk about religions as such, thus establishing a form of respect and non-interference in purely religious affairs. The party is not interested in religion, but it values the positive social contribution of religious people.

2 Here is the entire passage, according to the official English translation: "4. Expand the patriotic united front and unite with all forces that can be united. Promoting harmony in relations between political parties, between ethnic groups, between religions, between social strata, and between our compatriots at home and overseas plays an irreplaceable role in enhancing unity and pooling strengths. Acting on the principle of long-term coexistence, mutual oversight, sincere treatment of each other and the sharing of weal and woe, we will strengthen our cooperation with the democratic parties, support them and personages without party affiliation in better performing their functions of participation in the deliberation and administration of State affairs and democratic oversight, and select and recommend a greater number of outstanding non-CPC persons for leading positions. Keeping in mind the objective of all ethnic groups working together for common prosperity and development, we must guarantee the legitimate rights and interests of ethnic minorities, and strengthen and develop socialist ethnic relations based on equality, solidarity, mutual assistance and harmony. We will fully implement the Party's basic principle for its work related to religious affairs and bring into play the positive role of religious personages and believers in promoting economic and social development. We encourage members of emerging social strata to take an active part in building socialism with Chinese characteristics. We support overseas Chinese nationals, returned overseas Chinese and their relatives in caring about and participating in the modernization drive and the great cause of peaceful reunification of the motherland."

At the meeting on the 18th, Congress explored the issue.
Two experts introduced the subject. One was Zhuo Xin-
ping, a specialist on Christianity from the Chinese Academy
of Social Sciences, and the other was Mu Zhongjian, scholar
on Confucianism from the Central University of Nationali-
ties. It seemed the party wanted two perspectives, one about
the new Christian faiths coming from abroad and one from
the country's own native tradition.

Hu presented some introductory remarks, reported in a
Xinhua article in Chinese[3], and it was indeed a historical event.

---

3 Here, there are the two reports, in English and Chinese, which are
quite different.

Xinhua News. Updated: 12-19-2007.

Chinese President Hu Jintao on Wednesday reiterated a policy of free
religious belief while stressing law-abiding management on religious
affairs and support to self-governance of religious groups. Hu, also the
general secretary of the Communist Party of China (CPC) Central
Committee, made the statement at a meeting of the members of the
Political Bureau of the 17th CPC Central Committee in their study on
religious issues at home and abroad.

"We shall fully carry out the Party's policy of free religious belief and
manage the relevant affairs in line with the law," he said. The Party and
government shall encourage believers of all religions to keep their patriotic tradition and contribute to the development of Chinese society
and unification of the motherland, he said.

China's management of religion would be based on human understanding, he said, adding mutual respect was a must.

"The Party and government shall reach out to religious believers in
difficulties and help them through their problems," he said. Hu also
stressed the training and promotion of religious professionals, saying
that the CPC would help and support religious groups to improve self
governance, voice the opinions of its followers and protect their legal
rights and interests. Since last year a number of training programs have
brought together religious leaders, theology teachers and officials with
religion-related government departments. They took courses on reli-

Two facts are extraordinary.

It was the first high-level meeting of the Party fully devoted on religion. That was a sign that Party leaders recognize the great political significance of religion in building a "moderate, affluent, and harmonious society." Religion is no longer an issue of public security that can be handed over to the police – it is a top social and political issue involving all aspects of society, and therefore, all Politburo members must be aware of it.

Secondly, in all of the Xinhua reports, there were no negative, derogatory remarks about religion, as one would expect to find discussing what the Marxist tradition regarded as the

gious knowledge such as history of world religions and ethics, as well as practical courses in management theories, psychology and law.

The CPC is atheistic but allows freedom of religious beliefs. China is home to 100 million religious faithful, largely Buddhists, Taoists, Christians, Catholics and Islamists. At the 17th CPC National Congress ending in late October, the Party for the first time in its history has mentioned the word "religion" in an amendment to its Constitution. To incorporate into its Constitution the principles and policies the Party has formulated for guiding efforts to strengthen the work related to ethnic and religious affairs, among others, is conducive to their full implementation and getting better results in the Party's work in this area, said a resolution on the amendment to the Constitution. The CPC recognized that religions are a constant for a long time in the Chinese socialist society, Hu said at Wednesday's meeting. To properly understand and manage the religious affairs was vital to the work of the Party, the peace and stability of Chinese society and the process to build a moderately prosperous society of all respects, he said. "We shall fully understand the new problems and challenges to manage religious affairs so that we can do it right," he said. As the host country of the 2008 Summer Olympic Games, China has promised to offer religious services for foreigners arriving for the Games. It is working on religious facilities at the Olympic venues with the help of the International Olympic Committee and referring to the practices at previous Games.

opiate of the masses. There are not even "ifs" or "buts" to indicate that the Party will handle religion with diffidence. The English version stresses that there must be freedom of belief, and in the Chinese version, Hu is quoted as saying that the Party must mobilize the positive elements of religion for economic and social development. Thus, religion can play an important role in realizing the "harmonious society" that is the new political goal of the Party.

Furthermore, Hu spoke at the conference, meaning that he and the Party deem this issue of top importance and not simply something to be delegated to the United Front or the CCPCC, the two bodies coping with religious affairs in the Party. His speech, which might circulate in internal meetings, will set the direction for handling religious affairs in the future.

This does not mean that the Party has converted to some religious belief or is going to do so. Religion is an instrument for governance. As Pan Yue bluntly put it in his essay, the Party wanted to learn how it can use religion to appease people, to enhance social stability, and to avert rebellions and revolutions.

The CPC understands this is a complex issue, but one with many potential positive social outcomes. In the late 1990s, an investigation carried out in some coastal regions found that the areas with more people converted to a religious faith had a lower rate of criminality – more religion meant less crime.

However, Chinese history tells Party leaders that religion is also an extremely volatile element. Major uprisings in the past were organized by religious groups. For instance, the Taiping, who almost brought to an end the Qing dynasty in the 19th century, were pseudo-Christians. Similarly, extreme radical Islam now mobilizes millions worldwide. Religion has to be handled with care, but it cannot simply be ignored or looked down upon like some kind of feudal leftovers.

6. Peace in the war-view

Military thought is an integral part of the Chinese philosophical tradition. Among the ancient classics, "military thinking" is present not only in the *Sunzi Bingfa*, but also in the work of Mozi, China's first really systematic philosopher and the first to mount an opposition to the Confucian school. Here we have the three chapters on *fei gong* (against offensive war), which explain why a State should not conduct offensive wars but only defensive ones. Furthermore, in Mozi, we have fragments of technical chapters on the preparation of city defense, meaning that these philosophers were not only thinking about war, but preparing practically for it.

However, since the beginning of philosophical thought in China, war was not simply an episodic clash of arms or a parenthesis in the normal unfolding of politics and diplomacy, as Clausewitz would put it many centuries later. War was "a matter of life and death for the State," as Sunzi said. In the military classics, there is an extended concept of war, so as to include overall state preparation for war.

Shangjun is the philosopher credited with helping to organize the Qin State (the State that eventually unified China in 221 BC) and who inspired Hanfei Zi, one of China's greatest thinkers. In Shangjun's work, the author presents the organization of the tax system, the tilling of the land, and the military levy as a unified concept: they are all integral parts of state organization and military preparation.

In fact, war is the main function of the State. In the *Sima Fa*, a volume on the philosophy of war compiled in early Han times but reflecting previous ideas, the author begins by addressing the matter of the benevolence of the Son of Heaven. That is to say that a good government or benevolent ruler is the necessary basis for waging a good war. He creates a system that citizens are ultimately willing to defend with their own lives. And a good government guarantees a good life for the families of those who die on the battlefield.

To sum up, war is a total concept that includes what goes before and comes after the actual clash of arms. We can see the same attention to war in modern thinkers like Qiao Liang and Wang Xiangsui in *Chaoxian zhan*, (War beyond the limits – Asymmetrical war, Beijing, 1999). Here the two authors explain that war is political thought: strategy that goes beyond the use of weapons and tactics in the battlefields. This reasoning is echoed in the Italian author and general Fabio Mini's *La guerra dopo la guerra* (*The war after the war*), where he explains that one must not wage war without considering the sort of peace one wants to achieve. These ideas also appear in Mao's thought, which deals with the issues of social contradictions and guerrilla warfare.

Seen through this lens, war – the conflict and competition of States – is wider than shooting between soldiers. It is reasonable to argue that States are always at war.

But by the same token – with respect to the Chinese principle of *yin* and *yang* – one can also argue that States can be always at peace, that actual clashes and bloodshed can always be avoided or minimized. In other words, if war is constantly being waged in many ways, then one can try to curb the wars in which millions die. Wars could be "waged" in the form of cold or soft wars, as Joseph Nye would have it.

But in order to resolve conflicts without bloodshed, communication is crucial.

Nevertheless even the understanding created by open channels of communication would still require, if not an impossibly unified world view, then a *lingua franca* of ideas.

This is, in a nutshell, the idea put forward by Zhao Tingyang in *Tianxia Tizhi*: it is necessary for the world to have a common *"tianxia view"*. *Tianxia* is not precisely a shared culture so much as a shared sensibility; it is a common understanding that we all live in the same world, and have to share some kind of common understanding and tolerance of each other's ideas. It is different from the concept of empire.

Generally speaking, States and statesmen have differing world-views. For instance, during the Cold War and World War II, states embodied strong ideologies, which compelled their people to fight for them. Or, in the case of World War I, warring states were motivated not by ideologies but by opposing national interests, and in their citizens' case by nationalism itself.

What is the situation now? Are we witnessing clashes of ideologies, worldviews, and civilizations? Can war be avoided? Here we should not be under any illusion: war has been with us for millennia and will accompany us into the future. But a common *tianxia* would help smooth over conflicts and avoid the kinds of misunderstandings that lead to war. It could lead to some kinds of agreement like the ones that forbid the bombing of hospitals during wartime.

What would be the content of a *tianxia* system? We can sketch the minimal requirements: market economies, freedom of enterprise. These elements, though not implying deeply shared values, make it possible every day for goods to travel form one side of the world to the other. Russia has such a system to a certain extent. Other groups, like radical Islamic movements or old-fashioned communist movements such as the new Red Brigades in Italy, appear to reject the concept of the value of a common market.

Chinese tradition could ameliorate the present difficulties in the world. In ancient times, China was not "China" for the people living there; it was "all there is under Heaven." The rest, what was not part of the Chinese world, was simply not under heaven and beyond the sphere of this world.

The West's encroachment has helped to form a new identity: that of China. This, in turn, has created a new sense of the relationship of the "Chinese" people with the rest of world. However, the ancient sense of history lingers, creating new challenges as China is driven to become the largest economy in the world or to expand the scope of "all there is under Heaven."

During China's imperial past, order (*zhi*) was easy to understand. It entailed the concept of peace, with all things in their appointed places. Disorder (*luan*) was chaos, disaster, and death. Merchants and other businessmen began, over time, to cause *luan*.

Things had no fixed place: the price of their goods would change with time and place; businessmen could become richer than the local mandarin and thus put in jeopardy the order of a society whereby the official had to be the richest and most powerful. But businessmen were a small necessary evil – containable, but impossible to eradicate – like secret societies or small scale peasant uprisings.

But business is different in modern society and in modern China. If business itself becomes an integral part of peace, encouraged as the driving force of development, and military might leads to greater stability for China in the international arena, then how can order and peace be said to exist at all? What kind of order and peace can be expected in a place of constant and growing business? How can we square this situation with the Chinese historical preference of *zhi* over *luan*?

In a world in which wars are minimized and pushed to the periphery, war becomes a form of large-scale policing. This new perception radically changes the idea of war. When wars were like World War I, the lines between peace and war were clearly demarcated. If war becomes a matter of policing rogues and criminals, then one is always at war, because there will always be criminals.

For these matters, a different international framework is needed. The old traditional UN will simply not work, as it is not working now. Yet, it is not clear what new structure should be established.

Similarly, if *luan* is an integral part of a new order that includes international business, we need a new political structure to manage this society, a structure that is different from the imperial past. Here things are somewhat easier: experience in the West has proven that democracy has been effective in preserving a large degree of order and stability while still encouraging economic growth. In China, there are many students of Marx who believe deep down in theis souls that economics and politics go hand in hand.

So, simply stated, if China wants to manage the turbo-capitalism it has ignited, it will need some strong political change. What the future will be is certainly not clear, but some form of democratization might be unavoidable.

7. Culture reorganized

All of these changes clearly mean that China's whole cultural universe is being shaken up and reorganized. This started at the end of the 19th century with the massive arrival and translation of Western knowledge from the original languages or from Japanese translations[4]. At that point, the traditional organization and categorization of knowledge – dating back to Sima Qian (ca. 145-90 BC) and his first historic account in the Shiji ("historic records") of philoso-

---

4 The following argument is largely drawn from Ge Zhaoguang's "Zhongguo sixiang shi" ("History of Chinese thought"). Shanghai, 2001, Vol 2, pp. 466-476.

phers and literature before the Han empire – fell apart. That is, 2,000 years of tradition had to be reshuffled and re-systematized. The study, for instance, of what were previously considered the "classics" (*jing*), "masters" (*zi*), and "historical records" (*shi*) had to be relabeled under the new code words coming from the Japanese: "philosophy" (*zhexue*), "historiography" (*shixue*), and "literature" (*wenxue*). What's more, as Ge put it, "It was as if what the past, which could not just simply be called the study of classics, masters, or historical records, could not longer hold the old grand unity. The study of the words and language of the classics became an independent subject, and it was granted the honorific title of 'science' [another new, imported word] and other contents of the written legacy started going into historiography, philosophy, or literature, as if the wholly body of the classics was ripped apart in the execution by five horses tearing the limbs of a cadaver. The study of the masters followed the same destiny ripped apart into philosophy, ethics, logic, and even physics or chemistry."[5]

It is hard to fathom the depth of the change and the seismic waves that rippled through society and individual psychology. The colorful and passionate language used by Ge (born in 1950, over one century after the first Opium War) reveals that this change still touches the very soul of the Chinese people, even now when libraries, mass media, and education from primary schools have been following the new Western classification for about a century. When reading the classics, the scholar still feels the holistic soul of the ancient Chinese world seeping through the pages. This vision, for instance, of the Yijing (The Classic of the Changes, also found transliterated as "*yi king*" or written as "*I Ching*") is almost

5   Ge Zhaoguang, op. cit., p. 476.

impossible to ignore whether or not one believes in the pro-
phetic powers of the book. Its language and way of thinking
has pervaded centuries of cultural tradition and still pops up
in proverbs. Its way of approaching problems, handling situ-
ations, and considering issues resonates with truth in the soul
of the Chinese reader. This truth is impossible to dismiss, as
it would be for us to dismiss the Greek and Roman tradition.
Even Christianity had to digest Green and Roman culture to
conquer the souls of that world, and Islam did so with Greek
culture when it stretched into the then Hellenistic lands of
Asia Minor or North Africa.

Then, we have a series of massive cultural problems. The
Chinese have reclassified their cultural world according
Western criteria and are still digesting the problems and trying to finds way to reconcile the old with the new – a process
that will take centuries. Buddhism took half a millennium
to be completely assimilated, and back then the pre-existing
Chinese culture was not as complex as the culture now em-
bracing the Western world.[6]

Now, it is clear to all Chinese that Western culture is the
root of wealth, success, development, and political survival –
it is the essence of modernity. When China embraced Western culture, as it has been doing since Deng's times, it began
growing; when it closed down, as it did under Mao, it sank
into defeat, utter poverty, and political collapse. So, there is
only one road to modernity and success – Westernification.
And the shorthand for Westernification is America. For this

---

6   One could argue that present advanced communications tools, includ-
    ing mass media and the internet, can make contact easier and more
    widespread, thus shortening the time of assimilation. But challenging
    assimilation, there is the huge difference between Chinese and West-
    ern culture, a gap wider than the one that in Buddhist times divided
    Chinese and Indian tradition.

reason, there are over 200 million Chinese people studying English (the results are often poor, but that is a different issue), and English is now being taught in primary schools.

Meanwhile their souls are torn between East and West, between old and new, and uncertain to which they should pledge allegiance. They are hoping that there is a way to have them both.

In the end the result will be that, as Chinese residents in the many Chinatowns of the world are showing: they will have both, one way or another. This is apparent also in the cultural language, which still uses old sayings like "*ming zheng yan shun*" ("when names are right speech is consequential"), drawn from the Analects of Confucius but also from "Pandora Box," a Greek myth that is one of the "topoi" of the Western world.

This will create another problem, this one for us as Westerners. Since the Romans assimilated Greek culture in the 3rd century BC, the Western world has never met a massive cultural challenge. Even in colonial times, other cultures were dismissively branded as inferior and were never the object of wholesale incorporation, as Romans did with the Greeks. There has been piecemeal curiosity and interest, such as being incorporated into the conferences of geographic societies, carried out with great erudition and the careful "scientific" dissection of foreign texts – as if they were insects. But that was it.

However, China's economic and political growth is leading the growth of all of Asia, and there could be a time in the not so distant future when the economic and political might of Asia – or even just that of China – could be as great or even greater than that of the entire West. The West will then have to try to come to grips with the newly Westernized Chinese culture. This will shake Western culture to its roots and its soul, perhaps as it has shaken the Chinese culture.

We might remember that we were already Sinicized at one point in the 17th and 18th centuries, when China appeared to the West as a model for development. Europe was coming out of the religious wars between Catholics and Protestants, and hyper-Catholic Jesuits provided inspiration to both camps with translations of Chinese classics and accounts of Chinese culture. Their work stirred massive changes in the West, in fields ranging from mathematics (Leibniz invented the binary numbers inspired by the diagrams of the Yijing) to politics (the civil service and the idea of officials being promoted on grounds of merit, not birth, came from China). It's possible that even the idea of the abolition of monarchy through a popular revolution was inspired by the Chinese idea of *ge ming*.

It might be helpful to remind the Chinese that the West they are conversing with was already Sinicized, in a way – some of the modern concepts they are adopting are remodeled versions of Chinese ideas. Conversely, the West, which could face a massive "Sinification," should remember that it was already Sinicized in the past, and that the present and future China is largely Westernized.

This Westernification is not just in the heads of a handful of pundits, it is also in everyday life, as those who have been to China have seen. The changes hit the sentiments and the basic feelings of the people.

Here a few examples.

8. Language changed

In the past century, China saw dramatic changes in the language, which is the one element that more than any other "made" and unified China.

It is hard to overemphasize the importance of language in the making of Chinese civilization. Western civilization recognizes itself through a body of "literary lore" that has been translated from language to language, moving from Greek to Latin to national European languages. At each passage, the lore may be slightly adapted. However, there are remaining monuments that hold present Westerners "accountable" to their past. These monuments, scattered all over Europe and the Mediterranean Sea, prove the continuity of the past into the present and impose architectural canons that can be reproduced in modern cities. The works give modern Westerners established ways to organize cities, their lives, and even space or the concrete relationship between humans and nature.

In other words, even without the same language, even forgetting the body of classic literature, the columns and the domes of Washington DC's buildings make known to the passerby the uninterrupted continuity between the USA and the SPQR.

But China's evolution was different. Each dynasty made a point of tearing down all the buildings of the former masters to erect new ones. This was possible because of the greater wealth in China compared to Europe after the demise of the Roman Empire. Even in rich renaissance Rome, the popes extracted the marble for their palaces from ancient Roman relics – it was cheaper to dig stone from the Coliseum than from mountains in Carrara.

China does not seem to have had this problem and has many times chopped down entire forests to construct splendid residences for its princes.

Continuity was guaranteed by a rich body of literary works. Those works were passed down through a strict education system geared to producing the best administrators for the state. The hope of social advancement or preservation pushed all Chinese to try their lot with education. There-

fore, even if they failed the harsh exams, everyone deeply absorbed the tradition and language. There was no advantage
in illiteracy: government acts were written down all the way
to the emperor who had to read and vet them.

Language did not play the same role in the West, where
the tradition since Alexander and Cesar was for great political leaders to be great generals earning their power with the
sword. True, the West recognized that the pen is stronger
than the sword (*calamus gladio fortiori*), but there were many illiterate kings in the Middle Ages who were assisted in
matters of state by learned clerics. The Roman Empire was
defeated by barbarians, highly literary Greece was won by
semi-barbaric Macedonians, and less-developed Romans
conquered sophisticated Hellenic kingdoms.

Chinese kings were masters of conspiracy and political
plotting. They were devisers of strategies who read extensive-
ly and were imbued with the Chinese literary tradition – but
they were not fighting generals. Even Mao, famous for his
interest in military strategy, left the actual command of op-
erations to Zhu De and others. Ideal generals were thinkers:
bookworms willing to lend their literary talents to the battlefield. They were people like Zhuge Liang in *Romance of
Three Kingdoms*, a wise and knowledgeable schemer. Zhuge
had read all the Chinese books and thus could assess the psychology of his enemy (born out of the same cultural tradition) and devise a strategy fit to defeat him.

In this tradition, the continuity of physical monuments
was not important; what counted was the language.

In the West, language was not unity. The Roman Empire
was bilingual, with Latin and Greek. The division carried on
in the Middle Ages, when the kingdoms were also bilingual,
using Latin for their official business and local languages for
everyday life. Unity in the political body was created by the

idea of blood contiguity among one "people" – the bond of belonging to the same "ethnos" – at least among the top echelons. This was true of the people of the Akropolis, of the Senate, or of the Germanic aristocratic warriors of the Holy Romanic Empire.

In China, unity came through the use of the same language, which carried a tradition and a system of education. Whoever could master the language and education was part of the "Chinese" polity, irrespective of ethnic origin. Thus, language was far more important than in the West. Furthermore, the largely ideographic written language was a fantastic instrument for keeping unity among people speaking very different natural languages. Chinese characters, largely indifferent to pronunciation, could be used in Japan, Korea, Vietnam, southern China, and northern China. People could keep their dialects and still understand each other. Written languages reflecting pronunciation, like Latin, faced considerable problems in adapting the written form once the oral form changed, as occurred in Europe during the Middle Ages. The Chinese language, conversely, could move along the centuries with only minimal change. And so did it, until the 19th century.

Early on, in the first centuries AD, a difference developed between literary Chinese (*wen yan*) and "simple word language" (*bai hua*). The differences between the two, though quite important, are minimal compared with changes that occurred in the 19th century. Facing the massive inflow of foreign texts and the resulting adaptations in thinking, China changed its language. It introduced Western-style punctuation, including the previously unknown practice of dividing text into paragraphs. Syntax, trying to mirror convoluted Western thinking, became more complicated, a change that was possible thanks to a new system of punctuation, which made clear the structure of the sentence.

Other major changes soon followed. The binding of many books and magazines abolished the old order of writing first from top to bottom and then from right to left. China began to adopt the Western style, writing first from left to right and then from top to bottom.

Furthermore, matching Western attempts to create standardized pronunciation, China developed various systems of sound transliteration for the characters. (This also meant having to teach adults Chinese from the scratch.) There are, for instance, the *Bopomofo method* (adapted from the Japanese *hiragana* and still used in Taiwan) and the *pinyin system* (which uses the Latin alphabet and has been adopted in the Mainland). These systems froze the official pronunciation, preferring one elocution over another for the first time. It also officially divided the country into different dialects and accents. Before the standardization of pronunciation, it was perfectly legitimate for scholars to express themselves in dialect. Even Mao, who promoted the standardization of pronunciation, spoke unashamedly with a very heavy Hunan accent. Radio and television have since contributed to unifying Chinese pronunciation, but important differences persist without much attention.

In contrast, in many Western countries, proper diction is very important, and people speaking with a vulgar, base accent are reviled.

In his drive for reforms, Mao went even further, going to the very heart of his culture, the Chinese characters. After playing with the idea of using Latin script for Chinese, he gave the green light to a widespread simplification of the Chinese script. The break was so significant that for decades Chinese intellectuals outside of China pointed at simplified characters as evidence of Mao's total betrayal of Chinese tradition.

Even old texts are being reprinted with modern punctuation and paragraphs that, for many reasons, are not totally faithfully to the originals but are a partial "translation." Expanding on Ge Zhaoguang's feelings, we can say that this change to the language was like putting the splinters of the executed body in a meat grinder.

The result is a totally different world. Yet, many things persist. In recent years, China has seen a surge in long TV series that have a narrative process similar to classic novels like *Shuihu zhuan* ("Outlaws of the Marsh" written in the 14th century by Shi Nai'an). Here, the story advances without a plot that leads to a cathartic moment of solution[7], a definitive end, as you find in Western novels, Greek tragedies, and products of the modern film industry. These TV series can spawn new episodes forever without an ending, but always projecting into an open future, like human history. It is a storytelling structure resembling *Shuihu zhuan*, with chapters that end while opening to the next development, and not like American TV programs, in which each episode is self-contained and self-concluded.

It is as if the thing coming out of the meat grinder still remembers the original body. But what it is this thing?

9. Houses-apartments

Tall belvederes and towers for the observation of enemies, hunting, or religious purposes (like Buddhist stupas) have an ancient tradition in China. Yet, houses and living quarters were flat, rising two or three stores at most. They were often next to the ground, and ideally protected by surrounding walls. No house could be higher than that of the local

---

7 For these concepts, I am indebted to discussions with Dr. Andrew Lo of the School of Oriental and African Studies at the University of London.

mandarin or than the residence of the emperor. In fact, since ancient times, tall towers were considered extravagant and therefore restricted. The prohibition against buildings taller than those of the officials reinforced this idea.

Even as late as the early 1990s, Chinese cities were flat. Beijing was an endless sprawl of houses, with the tips of a few old Song-dynasty stupas spiking the horizon here and there, as if only Buddha and his holy men could reach for the sky. A decade later, the skyline of Beijing – and of every Chinese city and even villages – has dramatically changed. Everyone is allowed to put up his own stupa or hunting tower. Skyscrapers have rapidly become a common feature in China, as if anybody can be higher than the officials or the emperor, anybody can be a Buddha, a holy man!

The philosopher Liezi in the 3rd century BC wrote:

"The towers and belvederes built upon their heights were all made of gold and jade, the birds and beasts living there were all spotlessly white. Trees of pearl and coral bore thick masses of flowers; their fruit was delicious to the taste, and those who are thereof knew neither old age nor death. The inhabitants all belonged to the race of demigods and immortals, and in countless numbers they would fly across to meet one another within the space of a single day or night."[8]

In this case, the Western model played a strange trick with the backdrop of Chinese traditional culture. The West opened the floodgates of ambitions and desires stifled for thousands of years: reaching for the sky, something formerly possible only to immortals.

8   Translation by Lionel Giles: http://www.angelfire.com/in4/alchemy2084/giles.html

Now, literally, golden towers made of Italian marble whiter than jade, crowded with imposing "roman pillars," and guarded by monumental stone beasts – lions larger than mythical dragons – dot every city. Anybody can have an apartment in these immortals' abodes, if he can afford it. And even if he cannot afford it, he can still live in a more modest apartment block that stretches quite a few meters above the ground.

The psychological change is immense.

In the West, tall buildings were traditionally for poor people. In ancient Rome, there was a prohibition against building what we now call apartment blocks that were higher than seven stories. There were many cases of tall buildings that caved in or collapsed. In buildings, plebeians would lead crowded lives, while patrician senators and generals enjoyed the luxury of one-story villas with gardens.

The pattern was followed in future centuries in the West: the poor had small badly built homes where families would live dangerously on top of each other, and the rich had large estates. The issue was resolved with the modern invention of steel and concrete technology, allowing the safe construction of towers hundreds of meters high. This made it possible for people with lower incomes to have good, although cheap, houses. It also made it attractive for rich people to live in apartments, which could be as luxurious as villas. Essentially, this created a real sense of middle class with people living in the same neighborhood, maybe in the same apartment block, in apartments not too different from one another, despite even large differences in income.

In other words, towers in the West had a leveling effect, cutting extreme differences and making everybody normal. In China, towers made everybody special and everybody immortal. One could say that in the end the result is the same:

everybody is equal. But actually, it is not an identical result – it is very different. In the West, towers humble the ambitions of everyone. In the China, they stir up aspirations. In a way, towers in China are similar to suburban houses are in the West. The houses may remind the inhabitants of the old villas, and it is like everybody has a villa, so everybody is well off.

Being immortal is about being well off, but it is more – it is also about being beyond any control, satisfied, happy, and unrestrained. But the apartments are modern and imported from the West with the philosophy of middle class still stuck to it. Will the Chinese living in modern apartment blocks become more like suburban Americans, people living in Manhattan apartments, or the immortals of their ancestors' dreams?

Meanwhile, the traditional culture of flat houses has been bulldozed away. Most ancient cities, dating back to early Qing times, have been demolished to make room to the new towers. Curiously, Chinese have preserved former colonial Western buildings – the houses of the British, French, Americans and even Italians – but not the houses of the Chinese. It looks as if, despite the official anti-colonial rhetoric, to modern China, the Chinese legacy is less important than Western contacts.

10. Dresses and Chineseness

In India, a country that was under the foreign thumb for three centuries and an outright colony of the British, men and women pride themselves on their own dresses and clothes. Men sometimes wear a suit and tie but not all the time. In Africa, a continent partitioned by European invaders, men and women wear their traditional clothes, and even when they don't, they often have suits with bright colors reminiscent of their original taste for vivid tints. Even in

Japan, a place that chose to modernize and Westernize to avoid colonization, although men have rigidly taken on the standard European three-piece suit, women still don the traditional kimono for important occasions.

In China, a country that was never a colony, traditional dresses have just disappeared. Before Chiang Kai-shek and Mao Zedong, men used to wear a Western-style military uniform, and women would put on Western dresses or gowns inspired by the traditional Manchu woman's dress, the qipao. But after World War II, even those women's dresses were forfeited. In China, women were encouraged to dress like men, with slacks and jackets covering their femininity, while men stuck to "Lenin suits."

With the reforms, men started wearing ties and suits, and women regained access to gowns and dresses. But traditional dress had disappeared. In the late 1990s, Hong Kong fashion designer David Tang invented a new line of products that adapted traditional Chinese designs to modern circumstances. But it has never become a fashion trend, because both Chinese and foreigners feel awkward wearing clothes that make them stand out in a crowd. Conversely, peasants coming to work in cities proudly buy new suits and wear them to the construction site – without even taking the tag off the sleeve. Qipao, meanwhile, are just a curiosity found attractive mostly by Caucasian women.

Dresses are not superficial. They are complex statements that affirm identity, aspiration, and integration into a group. No 1960s rebel would go to an antiwar demonstration in a suit, a tie, short hair, and a bowl hat. Now, sporting long hair and jeans in a high-tech company means freedom and innovation, a look that is contrary to the suits and ties of Wall Street traders. Meanwhile, the orderly suits on Wall Street signify reliability.

Just looking at appearances, we see that Chinese people have forsaken their past and do not feel at ease going back to it. They want to become Westerners even more than the Japanese because do not have a mother or a wife in a kimono reminding them of their origin from the mythical goddess Amataratsu, mother of the nation.

It is a superficial statement, but Chinese believe that everything is on the surface. Everything about our characters and destinies is written on our faces. According to traditional "*shouxiang*" (reading of the face), a crease on the cheek or around the eyes reveals an aspiration and fate. But all that is unintentional. The intentional choice of dress is even more important and revealing because it is done to achieve a goal: to appear in a certain way for the purpose of looking Western and modern.

This abandonment of old "Chineseness" can be very Chinese. The concept and word for nation and nationalism (*minzu zhuyi*) came from the West. This is strong evidence that we are facing a very different concept of "nation" when we speak to Chinese people.

Even the names Chinese use for themselves are not consistent. They call themselves "*huaren*," an old term meaning "civilized people." The term implies that those who can speak "Chinese" and behave "Chinese" are "Chinese." That is, they are "civilized people" (*huaren*), regardless of blood origin. The only other example we can find of this concept and attitude is in America, with its policy of integration of all immigrants.

However, that was an old concept, and it different from that of *Zhongguo ren*, the people of Zhongguo (the "middle kingdom"). This term is geographical, implying all people who in live in China, including Tibetans, Uhigurs, and Mongols.

In China, the idea of an unparalleled civilization was so strong that it divided the world in civilized (*hua*) and uncivilized (*yi*). This vision came to an end with the maps of Matteo Ricci, which showed for the first time that China was not the whole world, that it was not even a great part of the world (*tianxia*), and that it was not the only civilization in the world. The people who drew those maps belonged to a world that could justifiably claim to be a civilization on China's level.[9] On those maps, the Jesuits called the land, which was only one part of the whole world (*tianxia*), "Zhongguo." The term was recovered from 2,000 years before, a move that significantly indicated that the states in the central plain hold the most ancient and truest form of civilization vis-a-vis the newcomers. Qin, Chu, Qi, and other states sat on the rim of the central plains. Ricci also reshaped the Western world map, putting "Zhongguo" in the middle to make up for the downsizing of its dimension, a change that had hit at the country's pride and vision of itself in the world.

Curiously, this massive cultural shock for the elite, as Ge Zhaoguang points out, coincided with the Manchu invasion. The invasion also marked the arrival of a foreign domination that tried to adapt to Chinese customs and made extensive use of Chinese officials, but that also kept its own distinctive characteristics.

It is important to consider that, according to Chinese tradition, the Manchu Qing dynasty came to power without usurping the existing power but by filling the void left from the failings of the previous Ming dynasty. It was an ideological campaign of legitimization, which was as important for

9   For a detailed discussion of the subject see Ge Zhaoguang's "Zhongguo sixiang shi" ("History of Chinese thought"). Shanghai, 2001, Vol 2, pp. 360-412.

holding on to power as was the military conquest. It came at a time in the 17th century when the political-military power of kings in Europe was reshaping their relationship with the religious-ideological power of the Church. Military and ideology, conversely, would remain the two levers of political power in China, a country in which, although the military remains the power of last resort, ideology commands military, and not vice versa.

There are also the Chinese abroad who call their Chinatowns "*tang ren jie*," the streets of the Tang (another dynasty) people. This is a curious phenomenon, since the Tang ruled China from the 7th century AD, and they were partly foreigners – their aristocracy was of Turkic origin, from the Tujue people living in central Asia.

Last, but certainly not least, there is idea of *han ren*, the people of Han (a weird idea – a nation named after a dynasty, as if the British were to call themselves the Windsors, or the Americans the Washingtons, or the Italians the Cesars). This nationalist notion was invented and used before World War II to stress the idea of a national war against foreigners, be it the Manchu dynasty, the invading Japanese, or the Western colonialists.

Countering the idea of a grand Han nationalism and of other people living in the "Zhongguo," the communists adopted the Soviet strategy of recognizing ethnic minorities and granting them a special status. This has created strange minorities like the "Hui" who are no different from the Han, except in their religious beliefs – they are Muslim. Should Christians and Catholics be granted the same status? Or should the idea of the Hui and the system of ethnic minorities be abolished? What would then happen to restive minorities who are uncomfortable with Han dominance, such as the Tibetans or the Uhigurs?

There cannot be just a piecemeal approach for China. China needs a broader set of values with which to think of itself and the world. These new values are currently non-existent. The Chinese economy has developed so far not because of a particular model, but because Chinese individuals are good at doing business and the government has not been hindering this trend.

But management of the new wealth, the new world, and the new development needs a new set of values. Ethics must go beyond the popular salutation *"gonxi facai"* ("wish you strike rich") offered at Chinese New Year celebrations. Laws, though important, are the minimal level of social contract – normal personal and social intercourse must find a course well above the minimal legal restriction, rather than just bordering illegality.

China is now in the middle of a lot of things and can go many ways. The issue for the next twenty years should be how to "groom" them – living with us Westerners and us living with them. This, more than anything, will determine our common fate.

11. A New World-view from China

Geography in the traditional Chinese world-view Feng Yulan, in his landmark work *History of Chinese Philosophy*, first translated into English in 1952, started from a geographical description of the conditions that gave rise to Chinese thought. Ancient Chinese philosophers were born on a large plain that shared a common language and culture. Tiny states, possibly concentrated around small towns, were expanding by conquering other neighboring states. The conquerors would try to manage the territory of the conquered better by fully integrating the vanquished population and land into a political and economic system unified with their own. Communication was very convenient along the existing roads linking different parts of a world that shared the same language and values. Thinkers and thoughts circulated widely in this humus as well, because there was a very concrete practical value in them – they provided a better means to make each ruler richer and stronger and thus helped each state to fend better for itself in times of conquest.

This environment was dramatically different from that of the Greek towns squeezed between the mountains and the sea. These cities were independent, did not create organized land states of the Chinese kind, but were largely trading posts. Here ideas were freely traded and discussed in the market place, alongside all other different goods, with potential 'customers', i.e. likely followers, competing thinkers.

Here the thinker wanted to 'win' an argument, that is, gain the support of the public listening to the debate as if they were at the theatre.

This was very different from China. Here we find the local philosopher talking most of the time to kings and rulers, trying to convince them that by adopting his theory the ruler's state will become stronger. The practical goal of the philosophical debate was so strong that Hanfei Zi, the master whose theory made possible Chinese unification with the first emperor, went so far as to reject the use of debate.

Yuqing made a house and told a carpenter, 'The house is too high.' The carpenter said, 'This is a new house, the mud is wet and the wood of the architrave is fresh.' Yuqing replied, 'It is not so – the wet mud is heavy and the fresh wood of the architrave is bent. The heavy mud cannot be sustained by the bent architrave, this will be proper when the house is lowered. After a few days the mud will be dry and the architrave will be desiccated. Dry mud is light and desiccated architraves are straight. To sustain light mud with a straight architrave, in this way it will be high.' The carpenter obeyed. He made it like that and the house collapsed.

Someone else said that Yuqing wanted to have a house made and a carpenter told him, 'The wood is fresh, the mud is heavy. If the wood is fresh it will bend; if the mud is wet it will be heavy; to sustain the heavy with the bent, even if it works today, in the long run it will necessarily be a disaster.' Yuqing replied, 'When the wood dries then it will be straight, when the mud dries it will be light. Now it certainly will become dry and after a few days it will be light and straight, and even after a long time necessarily there will be no disaster.' The carpenter obeyed, made it, finished, and after a while the house as expected collapsed.

Fanqie said, 'In the case of the breaking of a crossbow it must be at its completion, not at its beginning. When an artisan bends the crossbow he has to keep it in the bow-last three nights and then put the string on, wait for a day and then start the trigger. This is having rules at the beginning and being violent at the completion. Then it will not break.' Fanqie said, 'It is not so. Place it in the bow-last for a day and then put the string on. Wait for three nights and then start the trigger. This is being violent at the beginning and having rules at the completion.' The artisan had nothing to say but when it was used, the crossbow broke.

Fanqie and Yuqing's words are beautiful in debates and make them win, but are against the truth of facts. The lords are persuaded and cannot stop them – this is how they are defeated. When one does not plan an orderly and strong result but revels in the sound of hairsplitting discussions and beautiful speeches, then one will turn down the gentlemen who have the art and trust to the ones who make houses collapse and crossbows break.

Thus in dealing with the affairs of the state the lords do

not even reach artisans and crafts-men building houses and bending crossbows. Being so the gentlemen are limited to the cases of Fanqie and Yuqing: make up empty talk which is useless and win; the truth of facts, which does not change, is confined. The lords thrive in useless debates and have few unchanging words – this is how there is disorder. Today the ones who act like Fanqie and Yuqing are not stopped and the edicts of the lords do not stop – this is the category of why aristocracy is defeated and artisans and craftsmen are considered the ones who know the techniques. They cannot practise their skills, thus houses break down and crossbows break.

The ones who know how to rule cannot perform their method and art so the state is in chaos and the lord in peril. (Hanfei zi: *Wai chu shuo zuo shang* [my translation]) Hanfei zi's influence is huge, as his ideas helped the first emperor to unify China under his rule. But he is also part of an ancient tradition starting as early as the first Mohists, in the 4th century BC. They all wanted to prove theories against reality. This was in a way very different from the Greeks, who also, like Plato and Aristotle, despised empty talk. But Plato and his peers wanted to search for an argument's validity in the pure, true realm of mathematics, which provided 'true' ideas. Hanfei zi simply asked: is the roof or the crossbow solid? Will the house collapse, or will the crossbow shoot? Behind these questions we can feel the ruler's interest wondering: is this theory going to make me powerful, or will it destroy my country? Feng suggests that behind these different attitudes there were the needs of two peoples. The sea-faring Greeks looked at the fixed stars to find themselves and the route home on the wide ocean. There were also farmers struggling with changing weather and vicious invading enemies, and trying to set up a system that could increase crops and protect from encroaching invaders. The

Greeks had no large bountiful plain land to protect from a motley array of possible invaders, and the invaders were challenged at sea.

The ancient Chinese world-view was landlocked, because to the north and west China had the desert, to the south it had the mountains and to the east there was the sea. In the middle there was very rich soil. Then the issue and the drive for philosophers and rulers was not to try to move beyond these hard geographical limits but to retain this solid agricultural welfare.

The welfare of the Greeks was in the sea, not their scarce land. It was in their searching for new trade, new ports, new bargains, trying not to get lost and so looking to the stars, to the strict rules of navigation. Solid, mathematical truths helped those sailors.

In China, in other words, there was no reason to believe the world counted, everything under heaven that really mattered was those plains locked between desert, mountains and sea. Quite early the Chinese ventured out of those plains. The Han, the dynasty following the unifying Qin, reached the Caspian Sea in the west, went as far south as modern Hanoi to 'pacify' the people of Yue (the modern name 'Vietnam' comes from the Chinese for 'the pacified Yue') and sent explorers to Korea and Japan. But nowhere in their vicinity did they find a place as rich as their plains to justify arguably a further extension of their rule. So the geography of China has remained roughly the same since the first unification.

This is totally different from the geography of the Western world's history. The Greek world included modern Greece, southern Italy and coastal Turkey, which is not now considered part of the Western world, and Greece itself was until recently called 'the near east'. Rome was centred around the Mediterranean sea, which after the 7th-8th century split in two: the Western, Christian world occupies the north and the 'Eastern', Muslim world holds the south. The split has been there for over a thousand years and there is no end to this in sight.

The West, child of Greece and Rome, has moved into previously barbaric lands in the north of Europe and to distant America. In itself, with this migration, the idea of the West is associated with a cultural tradition, not a land. In a way this was consistent with the ancient ideas of Greeks and Romans, who remained Greeks and Romans regardless of the place they inhabited.

In China cultural tradition and land stayed the same and together for centuries.

Only recently have the Chinese adopted the ancient Roman habit of bringing 'China', building China-towns, where they live. But this possibly occurred because of cultural changes that started four centuries ago.

A new world – no longer under heaven Ge Zhaoguang, in his classic *Zhongguo sixiang shi* (History of Chinese thought, Shanghai, 2001, Vol. 2 ch. 13), explained the dramatic change in world-view brought to the Chinese court with the maps drawn by Matteo Ricci. Ricci had arrived in China years before. He learned Chinese, donned Chinese robes, took on Chinese manners. At the time this was enough to make him 'Chinese', which at that period was called *hua ren* (flowery man, civilized man). Foreigners (barbarians) were called *yiren*. At the time it was enough to become fully integrated in Chinese society, which did not recognize races and ethnic origins, but only cultural upbringing.

But at this point, according to the reconstruction by Ge, the sinicized Ricci said to his Chinese friends: Thank you for calling me civilized, as I am actually civilized, but I do not belong to your civilization but a different one. This sparked the emperor's curiosity. He knew of the rest of the world, he knew of other people, but he thought no other people had the level of civilization of the Chinese. So he ordered new maps to be drawn by Ricci.

This Ricci did according to the knowledge of the time. His first challenge was to save China's face. The emperor called himself the son of heaven and his empire was simply 'everything under heaven', *tianxia*. Ricci had to show not simply that China was not everything (which the emperor knew) but also that its territory was considerably smaller than the Chinese thought. He tried to compensate for this by putting China at the centre of the map, thus cutting the globe at the Atlantic Ocean, and christening China, not *tianxia* but *zhongguo*, the middle kingdom. The term had previously been used in ancient times, before the first emperor's unification, to indicate the kingdoms sitting in the middle of the Chinese plains. It was also used later, in Song times, to indicate the Song realm when the northern barbarians were pushing the Song court southwards. But with Ricci it took on a completely different nuance.

When the empire was strong and occupied the plains it was *tianxia*, because it ruled everything that mattered. Now Ricci was showing a different world, of which China was only about 5 per cent; this could still be called *tianxia* for ideological purposes, but it was really at best the 'middle kingdom'.

A different era was dawning for China and the world. Ricci died in Beijing in 1610; Shakespeare's death came just six years later. At that time the power of England was coming of age, after its victory over Spain, yet Shakespeare, interpreting no doubt a common feeling in England at the time, thought that Venice was the centre of the world. He set many of his plays in the Republic of Venice, for instance *Othello*, *Romeo and Juliet*, *The Merchant of Venice*. Shakespeare was not far from the truth. Despite the discovery of America the Mediterranean was still the centre of the Western world and here Venice was the linchpin of the sea's security and economy. Just a few decades before, in 1571 at Lepanto, Venice had led a Christian fleet that stemmed the invading Turkish forces. If the Turks had won at Lepanto, Europe might have been unified under Istanbul and, who knows, the Turks could have reached London by 1610 or 1616. Yet after its victory Venice began a rapid decline. The centre of the world and its trade became the Atlantic, with an increasing flow of products reaching Europe from America.

As a new world was starting for Europe, in a similar fashion a new world was starting for China at the time of Ricci's maps. Not long after his death, the Ming emperors were replaced in 1644 by the Qing, invading 'barbarians' from the north who retained and promoted the Jesuits who had reached China following Ricci. By the 18th century the Jesuits had become a force to be reckoned with in the imperial court. They held important offices with Fathers Von Schall and Verbiest, while another Italian, Giuseppe Castiglione (Milan 1688 - 1766 Beijing), was promoted court painter, and from there proceeded to change further the Chinese way of looking at the world.

Castiglione is famous for being the first to introduce the use of perspective into Chinese painting. Yet he did not simply paint according to Western methods, he adapted himself and Western perspective considerably to Chinese sensibilities. His paintings had no *punto di fuga* (vanishing point), a concept well known and widely used in the West since Da Vinci. Nor did they have the shading of light that had reached fantastic levels since the Venetian paintings of Tintoretto and his followers.

They did have a deep knowledge of anatomy, the working of the body beneath the clothes, and the bodies of animals, horses especially. In more than one respect Castiglione invented a new way of representing reality in a picture, something that was acceptable to the Chinese viewer. It was palatable for his immediate public, but nevertheless brought new elements to the representation of reality.

The role of court painter, and of court painting, is hard to assess in a world with TV, cinema and the Internet. Yet, in a world without moving images, without photography, court painting could be considered the one official way to represent reality, and thus to show the public how the court wanted reality to be seen, how the emperor wanted to show himself and his actions. In other words, next to the work of the official historian, court painting was the official representation of how reality should be seen. In this way Castiglione contributed to changing the way the empire wanted to show itself. The influence of Western perspective and sensibility went on to influence the building of the imperial summer palace of Yuanmingyuan, and even the design of some imperial gardens.

In all these artistic representations Western sensibility trickled into Chinese sensibility, creating something new and different. However, this new sensibility was consistent with the original Chinese one; it was not a total break like the one that occurred over a century later with the arrival of Western knowledge.

Perhaps never before had Chinese history experienced such a massive shock.

Buddhism had radically changed China over fifteen hundred years before, but it had done so over a period of a few centuries, a time when China also helped to change Buddhism and adapt it to its own habits and customs. This time Western knowledge took China by storm and in a few decades changed everything from language to systematization of knowledge, modes of dress, family structure and houses. It brought total change. Nothing was to be the same again. For millennia Chinese knowledge was organized into *shi*, history, *wen*, literature in a very broad sense, *zi*, the classical masters, *jing*, the classics. The West introduced a totally new system and totally new categories: philosophy, economics, sociology, etc. Of these some, like philosophy or logic, were ancient concepts, others, economics and sociology for instance, were new.

The new concepts were somehow easier to cope with: the new cultural production had to follow the new Western rules. But old Western concepts, like philosophy or logic, required the Chinese to look back at their own tradition and re-organize their previous knowledge into new categories. New words had to be invented, some craftily coined according to the meaning of the original Chinese characters, like *zhexue*, philosophy; others were so new that translators could not help but just borrow the sound, so 'logic' became *luoji*. Accordingly, armed with *zhexue* and *luoji*, the Chinese had to look back to their past and find their own history of 'philosophy' and logic. In a way the whole Chinese past had to be reconsidered in the light of the present. Chinese tradition was used to some extent in this exercise. Any new dynasty would write the history of the previous dynasty to set its own records straight. But it was a small attempt, as historians had to handle two or three hundred years of history and had the task of finding continuity between present and past. In a way then the present had to conform to the past.

The cultural revolution of the late 19th century and in fact all of the 20th century in China was (and still is) much wider. It does not want to have the present conforming to the past, on the contrary it wants to re-read over three thousand years of past history according to present necessities and sensibilities. These sensibilities are largely, if not totally, Western. In a way China was forced by circumstances to look back at herself through different eyes – Western eyes. The effort of conversion went so deep that it engulfed almost every aspect of life. Traditional ideal families, with many wives and crowds of children, gave way first to one-wife families then even to single-child families. Homes, which ideally developed horizontally in a sequence of courtyards and pavilions, now developed vertically in apartment buildings. The traditional imperial system, which had lasted for millennia, was replaced by a republic that crowned a handful of foreigners (Marx, Engels and Lenin) as its inspiring force.

In other words, for over a century China looked at herself through new, foreign lenses and thus did not have any real ambition, or even time and will, to develop a fresh look onto the new world outside. In ancient times it did not, because it had little or no interest in the outside world, later it not have the time and energy.

But China's growing economic and political role in this century forces her to develop, for the first time in her history, a really global world-view. In this sense the first systematic effort by Zhao Tingyang is special. He does it by drawing inspiration from ancient Chinese history. The present world looks to Zhao similar to that of the Springs and Autumns period, between the 8th and 5th century BC. Then there were many states, *guo*, competing with each other. Some were far more powerful than others and vied to gain the power to be the 'hegemon', *ba*. At the same time there was still the person of the 'son of heaven', *tianzi*, who was devoid of any real power but still retained an important ceremonial influence. It was a situation possibly similar to that of medieval Japan, where powerful fiefs fought over the right to become *shogun*, the main driving power in Japan, while the emperor was relegated to a largely ceremonial role. But the victory of one *shogun* or one *ba* did not eliminate all other fiefs or states.

Or it was similar to late medieval Europe, where many states were competing for power and the pope retained a religious role of mediation between them.

Nowadays there is no Japanese emperor, no medieval pope, no son of heaven to mediate between competing states and bestow his blessings on the winner. But there is a situation of competition among states and there is the need to establish a common language, a common understanding among them, similar to the one China had during the Springs and Autumns period, argues Zhao Tingyang. At the same time Zhao appears concerned about the emergence of possible 'hegemons' whose power could be unrestrained, as there are no mediating figures, like the son of heaven, and international organizations like the UN are very weak.

Besides the political, practical consequences one can draw from Zhao's analysis, there is perhaps an even more important consequence. After decades of looking at the world through the lens of the history of Greece and Persia, of the Roman Empire, Zhao offers to a world public the lens of a particular period of Chinese history to see modern reality. This in turn encourages a wider knowledge of Chinese history, beside Western history, that will also influence the global world-view.

In this way Zhao actually makes evident what was a 'hidden' reality: that, despite over a hundred years of intense westernization, Chinese travelling, doing business, talking about world politics, look at the world according to protocols that are different from those used in the West. However, re-read according to Western criteria, Chinese history and philosophy have a thrust that is very different from that of Western history and philosophy. After these hundred years of westernization China is different from its past, but it is still China, and it will not become another Western country.

This effort is necessary for China and for Asia, as the Thai thinker Pansak Vinyaratn said to us, analyzing the present situation in the region. Asian countries, he argued, need a sophisticated intellectual system underpinning their dealings with the West. This intellectual system should also underpin a modern management capacity and the efficiency of the economy. As Pansak argues, only China is moving in the direction of building this system; in other Asian countries there is only chauvinism under a veneer of modernization. Asian countries need this system to balance what from Asia look like two separate intellectual forces – continental Europe and the Anglo-Saxon world, the US and Great Britain.

The practical consequences of this – as we are speaking of China and we want to be practical like the Chinese – could be huge: families, homes, clothes, despite their apparent Western flair, retain and will retain an important Chinese content. And so in a way the world, and in this case the West, will also have to learn to become a little Chinese.

12. Chinese globalization

Globalization in the West started with the Greeks – with the Anabasis told by Xenophon, a disciple of Socrates. Then, 10,000 Greek mercenaries marched to Persia to aid Cyrus, who enlisted Greek help to try to take the throne from Artaxerxes. This occurred between 401 BC and March 399 BC. About half a century later, Alexander the Great (356-323 BC) followed almost the same route not to serve the Persians, but to battle and defeat them. He wanted to conquer and discover new lands, following the legend of the trials of Hercules. Alexander and his conquests then became the model for great Roman conquerors: Cesar and the emperors following him. Exploration, conquest, and plunder were the trademarks of the Mediterranean world, where the line between commerce and pirating was often blurred. Exploration and conquest were the driving forces pushing Spanish and Portuguese ships across the Atlantic in search of new sea-lanes to the Indies. The Atlantic was an extended version of the Mediterranean[10]. It was a space to conquer and win – seeing it as a limit would be an admission of defeat. The colonial era and present globalization are modern adaptations of the old principle of expansion. In each era, the idea was that economic welfare could be achieved through goods from new conquered lands, which were obtained through plunder, exploitation, or simple commerce. Security was best achieved by attacking enemies first and invading their lands, before they did the same, an action that was also rewarded by the booty of plunder.

In China, everything was different. Desert and mountains in the north and the west, jungles in the south, and the ocean in the east were the natural limits of conquest. In 200 BC, the first unification of China defined what is still the reach of Chinese civilization. The first emperor had conquered what is now northern Vietnam and had probably gone as far as present North Korea. The conquest of the wild south proceeded slowly and methodically, in a spirit of systematic incorporation into the empire. The empire stretched out to fight the warring barbarians and moved several times as far as the Caspian Sea or northern Siberia, but it always withdrew from it. The idea was that the security of the empire would be guaranteed by a belt of buffer-vassal States. In return for their "service," these States received from the empire more than what they offered as homage.

---

10 For an extensive treatment of the issue, see the first chapters of Feng Youlan's History of Chinese Philosophy (rev. ed., 1952-53).

The world outside was known and could be explored, as in the famous 15th century Zheng He expeditions, but it was of no major consequence for the empire, which had to produce security and economic welfare from within. Agriculture was fundamental to the growth of necessary industry, but there was no trust in the benefits of bouts of plunder and conquest. This was the way of the northern population or eastern pirates, but both did not make a stable living out of these activities and often survived on the verge of extermination. It appeared much better for the empire to improve domestic agriculture, industry, and trade. Industrial and agricultural surpluses in ceramics and tea drew in furs and horses (the latter necessary for the industry of defense) from the north or gold and silver from the western traders. China could easily ignore the rest of the world, because it was not relevant.

This changed dramatically after the Opium Wars, when England tried to sell the only goods China would consume and import – drugs, specifically, opium – to make up for a massive trade deficit that was draining Europe of all its American silver and gold. When China restricted the trade of opium on grounds that presently seem more than reasonable – it was drug trade, after all – England forced the trade to continue by fighting and winning a short but momentous war.

Over a century later, the lesson China learned is that even defeat in a small-scale war can trigger a deep political crisis, which in turn can topple a government.

Most importantly, the wider lesson is that China cannot ignore commerce and must be part of the global economic cycle, which now is highly industrialized and demands more resources than can be found internally. Therefore, China must go around the world looking for all kinds of resources and energy as well as new markets for its growing industries.

In other words, China as a State[11] recognizes the same economic necessities that Western countries have addressed for centuries, if not millennia.

Western States have refined, through centuries of experience and mistakes, the methods and practices for dealing with foreign countries that are used even now. China's methods for dealing with foreign lands are largely useless. It cannot rebuild a belt of vassal States – neighbors would bitterly resent China and turn against it. China then has to go to places where it traditionally had no foreign policy, for instance Africa and Latin America, without knowing well how to handle these people. In other words, the old foreign policy must be rejected, and there is no culture or experience for the new foreign policy.

It is a brave new world for China. And for the world, it is a brave new China.

11 For centuries there were Chinese traders in Southeast Asia, or migrants to America, but their activities were of no concern to the Chinese State.

Contents

www.ingramcontent.com/pod-product-compliance
Lightning Source LLC
Chambersburg PA
CBHW032054040426
42449CB00007B/1103